GOD
BREAKS HIS
SILENCE

A Study Guide for
CHRISTMAS

GOD
BREAKS HIS SILENCE

A Study Guide for
CHRISTMAS

t411.com

Truth411
HOUSTON, TX

 LUCIDBOOKS

CONTENTS

BEFORE YOUR BEGIN

The air is getting colder. The days are getting shorter. Fall is here and Christmas is coming. The stores have already prepared their windows, the neighborhoods are decorated with wreaths and lights, and the kids are excited.

Everything about this time is grand. Andy Williams was right: it is the most wonderful time of the year. From the Christian's perspective, this time is particularly special because we celebrate the coming of our Lord, Jesus. Beyond the Santa exploits and arguments over nativity displays in public, there is a culminating atmosphere that directs all of our senses toward Christ.

It has become easier each year to forget what the season is all about. There's the hustle in buying, the traffic in the streets, and that irritated lady who mouths off to the store clerk when they run out of Elmos. So many things can distract us from—pardon the cliché—the reason for the season.

If we can prepare ourselves ahead, this time of the year can be wonderfully useful to our families. We have to be intentional. We have to take advantage of the sights, sounds, and smells, and use them to stir our affections toward heaven.

This short study guide is aimed at doing just that. It focuses on two different stories about two different people from two different cities who respond two different ways to one similar message— salvation is coming. We look at Luke chapter 1 to see how the angel Gabriel interrupted a common man's priestly duties in Jerusalem to announce the herald of Christ. Then, we will travel about 60 miles north to Nazareth to see how Gabriel interrupted a common girl's daily routine to announce the Son of God. Finally, we will compare the two stories and close with Mary's Magnificat, her famous song of praise.

Additionally, you will find some articles toward the back of this short book that correspond to the lessons. If you are a discussion guide leader, it may be helpful to read the article that correlates with the lesson before you begin. It will help you better understand the story and the lesson objective. It might also give you some tips on how to facilitate an effective discussion. Finally, there is an introduction immediately after this that will set the stage for the first lesson and the lessons to come. Be sure to read it individually or collectively with your small group before beginning.

If saying "Merry Christmas" to the cashier who responds "Happy Holidays" doesn't spoil your joy, then you will appreciate this study. It brings us face-to-face with the Word of God and asks, "How will you respond?"

GOD BREAKS HIS SILENCE

FOR BIBLE STUDY

"Long ago, at many times and in many ways, God spoke to our fathers by the prophets, but in these last days he has spoken to us by his son."

—Hebrews 1:1-2

INTRODUCTION

"in these last days
God has spoken to us by his Son"

HEBREWS 1:1

The "silent treatment" can be brutal. We've all experienced it before. Some of us have dished it out. It's what happens when you upset someone so much that to speak would be the end of you.

The Israelites experienced it as a nation. God was silent for several generations, not because He was angry, but because He was rolling up His sleeves preparing the greatest speech in human history —the incarnation of the living Word.

The Israelites had a long past with God's Word. He spoke to them through clouds, bushes, fire, prophets, patriarchs, kings, and more. The writer of Hebrews said, "Long ago, at many times and in many ways, God spoke to our fathers by the prophets, but in these last days he has spoken to us by his Son" (Heb. 1:1-2). With the appearing of Jesus, we have God's ultimate self-expression. "He is the radiance of the glory of God and the exact imprint of his nature," Hebrews continues (Heb. 1:3). When Jesus was born, God spoke most powerfully.

But our story begins several hundred years before Christ. The gospel had been unfolding since God's promise concerning Eve and the serpent in the garden some 4,000 years prior (Gen. 3:15). But rather than eagerly anticipating the promise fulfillment, the nation of Israel had grown spiritually cold. Their obedience had evolved to ritualistic chores and their affections had turned toward the world. "Why are we wasting our time serving God?" (paraphrased, Mal. 3:14). They had failed to give God their heart.

The story of God's redemption was grinding to a climactic halt. Malachi captured the Lord's shocking words:

> "Behold, I will send you Elijah the prophet before the great and awesome day of the LORD comes. And he will turn the hearts of fathers to their children and the hearts of children to their fathers, lest I come and strike the land with a decree of utter destruction." (Mal. 4:5-6)

Then, God goes silent.

Those were the final words of the final book of Scripture. It was a frightening cliffhanger. God was sending a herald to prepare the hearts of the people so that when the Lord came, He would not wipe them all out for their hard hearts. And swiftly, God hushed … for 400 years.

Despite the warning, things continued spiraling downward as you would expect. Typically when the teacher is gone, the students act badly. The Israelites were no exception. It's no wonder God sent someone to prepare the way for His holy Son.

The wait was tough. Israel had grown accustomed to God's interaction. But He had not miraculously intervened in 800 years. No angels had appeared in 500 years. And now, no prophet had spoken for 400 years. It was all crickets for the Jews.

God was not stubbornly quiet to spite His people. He hadn't run out of things to reveal. He didn't get distracted or lose His tongue. He purposely withdrew Himself for His own purposes.

But now, He was about to break His silence.

"He will turn many of the children of Israel to the
Lord their God, and he will go before him in the
spirit and power of Elijah, to turn the hearts of
the fathers to the children, and the disobedient to
the wisdom of the just to make ready for the Lord
a people prepared."

—Luke 1:16-17

WHEN GOD SPEAKS, WE SHOULD BELIEVE

"How shall I know this?"

LUKE 1:18

It was a bloody mess. Blood on the floor. Blood on the walls. Blood on the garments. Jews from all over the known world were coming to the temple, as was their custom, to offer animal sacrifices to God—a picture to prepare them for the Messiah's work on the cross.

The priests would receive the animal and butcher it, separating specific parts of its body for specific purposes of worship in the temple. It would be burned, poured over coals, and surrendered to God in prayer. It was a scene of death.

There were about 18,000 priests at that time, divided across 24 divisions. Twice a year, a division would serve seven days in the temple. Doing the math, 750 priests were performing their duties on any given day. Out of those, only one would be privileged to carry the bloody, burning coals into the Holy Place. They drew straws to choose that person. It was the opportunity of a lifetime, literally. A priest could enter the Holy Place only once.

Our story introduces Zechariah. He is that privileged priest, that randomly chosen, insignificant man who just happened to be doing his job the day God broke His silence. He was a common man. In fact, he was one of 18,000 priests who were just like him. On the surface, there was nothing extraordinary about him being chosen for the job. It was in the straws.

OPENING THOUGHTS

1. Read Luke 1:5-25 and discuss your initial thoughts. What do you find most notable about Zechariah's encounter with the angel?

2. How would you have responded to Gabriel's appearance and announcement? Would you have believed him? Why or why not?

A COMMON PRIEST

Nothing about Zechariah was extraordinary. The Bible tells us he was an old priest with no children—which made him a sham of a man among the people (Ps. 127:3). He was one in a million, but in a bad way.

In God's opinion, however, Zechariah and his wife, Elizabeth, were "righteous before God" (Lk. 1:6). This meant they didn't simply go through the motions of worship. Their hearts were in it. They were "Old Testament Christians," you might say.

Priests who entered the Holy Place would dress in a robe with bells that would ring with each step he took. A rope was tied to his ankle. The idea was if the bells stopped ringing, the priest was assumed dead and could be dragged out by his foot. Those who offered the sacrifices would gather around outside to pray until the priest returned.

3. How do you think Zechariah felt going into the Holy Place for the first (and only) time? How do you think it influenced his reaction to Gabriel?

4. What do you think the priests and families outside were thinking as they prayed and waited? Do you think the sound of the bells changed in any way to alarm them?

5. Why do you think God chose such a common man?

6. Name other "common" men or women chosen by God in the Old Testament. What methods did God use to inform them?

An Uncommon Word

Zechariah was a common man, just like you and me. Being a priest was nothing extraordinary. He didn't work his way into the priesthood. He was born into it. He had no choice, neither was he awarded the duty of offering in the Holy Place. God picked a common man for an uncommon purpose—to receive an uncommon word—and broke His silence.

Typically, people did one of three things when they encountered an angel: they died, they ran, or they feared deeply. The Holy Place had only one entrance. Gabriel could not have been a man who just "appeared" inside. So upon seeing him, Zechariah was troubled. He wondered if the bells on his robe were about stop ringing.

7. How did God break His silence? What did He say and why was it significant?

8. Describe Zechariah's response to Gabriel. Why was it so hard for him to believe?

9. Have you prayed for something and waited years for God to answer? How has waiting shaped your faith?

10. What can you apply to your life from Zechariah's story? Are you willing to believe God's Word despite contrary circumstances?

CONCLUSION

Zechariah, physically and emotionally drained, from years of priestly duties and unanswered prayers for a son, disbelieved God's Word. As a result, the angel struck him mute and deaf (Lk. 1:62-63), a serious punishment for a man who wanted to tell all about his wife's pregnancy.

How do you typically respond to God's Word? Remember, Hebrews 1:2 tells us God speaks to us today through His living Word, and it is no less significant than if it came from an angel directly to you. Whenever and however God speaks, it is always Scripture. With the coming of Christmas, consider your response when God speaks—is it belief or disbelief?

_____

_____

_____

_____

_____

_____

_____

_____

_____

_____

_____

_____

_____

_____

_____

_____

_____

_____

_____

_____

_____

_____

_____

_____

_____

_____

_____

_____

_____

_____

_____

_____

_____

_____

_____

_____

_____

_____

_____

_____

_____

_____

_____

_____

_____

_____

_____

"He will be great and will be called the Son of the Most High. And the Lord God will give him the throne of his father David, and he will reign over the house of Jacob forever, and of his kingdom there will be no end."

—Luke 1:32-33

WHEN GOD SPEAKS, WE SHOULD TRUST

"How will this be?"

LUKE 1:34

The wind blew gently that afternoon as it did so many others. Nothing about it was extraordinary. It was just a usual day full of usual happenings. A young Jewish girl named Mary was grinding wheat and barley into flour, preparing food for the evening. Her father was off to work, her siblings tending to chores, and her mother away at the market.

Although alone at the house, no one was concerned about her safety. It was a small town with little noise, only the sound of young children playing and running about. There were only 2,000 souls in the whole city. You could easily miss it passing by in a caravan. Luke referred to it as Galilee. People knew Galilee. But this place, Nazareth, where was that?

Israel had not heard from God in 400 years. There had been no angelic appearances in 500 years, and no miracles in 800 years. Not until sixth months ago when Gabriel appeared to Zechariah, gave him God's Word and a miraculous conception. Now, on this usual day in this usual city as this usual girl was tending to her usual chores, God would do it again. This time, an even more miraculous conception would occur.

OPENING THOUGHTS

1. Read Luke 1:26-38 and discuss your initial thoughts. What do you find most notable about Mary's encounter with the angel?

2. How would you have responded to Gabriel's appearance and announcement? Would you have believed him? Why or why not?

A COMMON GIRL

"Can anything good come out of Nazareth?" Nathanael asked, when Philip told him about Christ (Jn. 1:46). Nazareth was such an agricultural place and not particularly known for anything good. It was plain. So plain that not even a fisherman thought anything worth while would come out of it.

Mary, a teenage girl, was the only thing competing with Nazareth for insignificance. She lived in it. Her four letter name was so common in her day that we have more than seven in the New Testament alone. Luke tells us Zechariah was "righteous before God" (Lk. 1:6). But of Mary, he only says she was a virgin (Lk. 1:27). In the same verse, Luke says more about Mary's husband-to-be than her.

When the angel appeared to this common girl, she was not in the temple performing dignified priestly duties. Rather, she was at home making dinner. No one was relying on her for any spiritual purposes, only the work of her hands. And there were only a few who needed that.

3. Given the social status of women in her day, how do you think Mary felt when the angel spoke to her?

4. What is the significance of calling Mary a "virgin"?

5. Do you think Mary's age affected her response to Gabriel's message? Why or why not?

6. As a teenage girl belonging to a Jewish family, what factors may have influenced Mary's belief system?

An Uncommon Word

Mary must have had her back to the angel when he spoke because it was his greeting that troubled her, not his appearance. "Greetings, O favored one, the Lord is with you!" This was not your typical "hello"!

Describing her as "favored one" was pretty significant. It didn't imply that she had or did anything in particular to warrant God's goodness. Rather, it implied that God, out of His goodness, wanted her to be favored. He intended to make her the mother of our Lord. Now that is significant!

God broke His silence yet again. This time, the word was that she would have a son and name Him Jesus. He would not be a common boy. He would be the "Son of the Most High" and "of his kingdom there will be no end" (Lk. 1:31-33). Gabriel explained how it would happen (Lk. 1:35) because nothing is impossible with God (Lk. 1:37). In this promise, Mary simply trusted. "Let it be to me according to your word," she said. No objections. No complaints. Mary trusted God's Word.

7. What message did Gabriel give Mary? Why is it so significant?

8. How did Mary respond to the Word of God? How was her response similar or different from that of Zechariah (Lk. 1:18)?

9. Why do you suppose the angel told Mary about Elizabeth's pregnancy? What practical lesson can you learn from their experience?

10. How has this lesson shaped your thinking about God's Word? Does it encourage you to have more faith in Scripture? Why or why not?

Closing

Mary, a lowly Jewish girl from an undistinguished town, modeled the proper way to respond to God's Word—with faith. Although she knew it was extraordinary, she trusted God to make possible the impossible conception of a child in her womb. She was graced by God to be favored for all time.

How do you respond to God's Word when you hear or read it? Do you trust in His promises when reality says otherwise? Do you stand confidently and lean into the unknown? God can do the impossible. When He says He will do something, He will do it because nothing thwarts His plan (Is. 14:27). With Christmas coming, consider how you will respond when God speaks—is it with doubt or faith?

"My soul magnifies the Lord, and my spirit
rejoices in God my Savior."

—Luke 1:46-47

WHEN GOD SPEAKS, WE SHOULD WORSHIP

"Why is this granted to me?"

LUKE 1:43

The excitement was too much. Mary left home as soon as she was able. Elizabeth was sixth months pregnant, and seeing Elizabeth would increase her faith and allow her to celebrate God's grace. Mary believed His word and trusted. She didn't need confirmation. She needed spiritual strength.

Unlike Elizabeth, whose reproach among people would be lifted by God's word, Mary knew that reproach was coming because she was unmarried and expecting a baby. Nevertheless, this was thrilling news. She needed to see her pregnant cousin.

This was an extraordinary time. Not only was the long anticipated Christ coming, He was making His way through these rather common people. The red carpet was being rolled out. But there were no cameras, no lights, no press conferences. There was only a mention in the ears of a virgin girl, an old man, and his barren wife.

Even in these trifling events, God broke His silence in a spectacular way. It was the first miracle in nearly a millennium, the first angelic appearance in half a millennium, and the first time God had spoken in several generations. It was all happening at once. And yet, it was nothing compared to the thunderous Word that would be born into this world.

OPENING THOUGHTS

1. What are some similarities between the two stories of Mary and Zechariah? What does it say to your heart at this moment?

2. What are some differences between the two stories? What do those differences teach us about ourselves and how we relate to God and His Word?

3. Read Luke 1:39-55. What stands out most? Why?

A COMMON NEED

The stories of Zechariah and Mary are strikingly parallel. Both involved common people being interrupted by an angelic visitation while doing their common duties. Both are greeted by Gabriel and deeply troubled. They were both told, "Do not be afraid," and both promised a son. The promised sons were both considered unusually great. Zechariah and Mary responded to the angel with questions. The angel gave them both signs, and both were extraordinarily blessed for the sake of blessing the world.

Mary, desiring to affirm and strengthen her trust, rushed to Elizabeth's house. And, while greeting her, baby John leaped in the womb—no doubt meeting his destiny as the herald of the Messiah. It was as if he was pointing and telling, "The Savior is here!" How could he do that? Because God said, "he will be filled with the Holy Spirit, even from his mother's womb" (Lk. 1:16).

His mother, exuding with joy and also filled with the Holy Spirit, realized what had happened and burst out a prophetic word of blessing. She blessed Mary, blessed Jesus, blessed herself, and blessed all who believe the Word of God (Lk. 1:42-45). Mary, also overwhelmed by it all, cried out in a song of worship, magnifying the Lord for His mercy and grace on the humble, His strength and might above all people, and for keeping His promise made 4,000 years prior.

4. How do you think this event strengthened Mary's faith and encouraged Elizabeth? Why do you think they needed it?

5. Why do you suppose Elizabeth, although needing a son "to take away [her] reproach among people," celebrated the faith of Mary and the coming of the Lord instead? How does this relate to your life?

6. How do you respond when God's promises are fulfilled in your life? Do other believers share your response?

7. Who was noticeably absent from this time of worship and celebration? How does his condition compare to others who doubt God's Word?

AN UNCOMMON WORD

The stories of Zechariah and Mary also had some differences. Some were more obvious than others. For instance, Zechariah was an old man. Mary was a young girl. Zechariah was married in need of a child. Mary was single and not seeking a child. Zechariah had a lifetime to cultivate his faith. Mary only had several years. Zechariah's promise would lift his reproach among people. Mary's would bring her reproach among people. Zechariah didn't believe. Mary did.

More subtle differences are found when you look more closely. Zechariah's son would be great among people. Mary's son would be the epitome of great. Zechariah's son would point to the Christ. Mary's son would be the Christ.

Mary and Elizabeth's shared joy was overwhelming. They were both caught up in adoration of the Lord. It was a spiritually rich time. Zechariah, made deaf and mute, would not have heard the loud bursts of his wife and cousin. So Mary followed Elizabeth's prophetic blessing with "The Magnificat," as it is commonly called today. It is the summary of the spirit of Christmas—the Lord's promised gift now given to the world.

8. What is the particular focus of Mary's song? Where does it lift her heart?

9. What words would you use to describe Elizabeth and Mary's response after having been assured of God's Word? What does this say to you?

10. Have you had similar moments where your heart was lifted to God for His good blessings and His great Word? How did you express yourself?

11. How has this lesson moved your heart to worship God this season? Does it encourage you to believe and trust Scripture more fully? Why or why not?

CLOSING

These are stories of common folk just like you and me. Some of us are old and bruised by life. We've prayed for decades and seen no end. We've concluded that God is still silent. We've wondered if God is able. We've lost the connection with God's Word. We see it as mere paper—not the culminating picture of Jesus. So we don't read it.

The Scripture is God's Word. The Scripture is where God speaks (Heb. 1:1-2). When our hearts grow cold and our lives become dull, we question His truths, dispute His gifts, and distrust His promises. The gospel of John describes Jesus as the incarnate Word of God, the Word made flesh, the climactic message of God, the divine self-expression. He existed before creation and was introduced into creation (Jn. 1:1-18). This is the birth of Christ.

When the written Word is read, the living Word is seen. This Christmas, how will you read God's Word? Who will you see come to life through Scripture? Who will take presidential focus in your family this season? Are you anticipating a profound break of silence as you reflect on the birth of the incarnate Word? How will you respond to the Christmas season?

_____

_____

_____

_____

_____

_____

_____

_____

_____

_____

_____

_____

_____

_____

_____

_____

_____

_____

_____

_____

_____

_____

_____

_____

_____

_____

_____

_____

"The Word became flesh and dwelt among us, and we have seen his glory, glory as of the only Son from the Father, full of grace and Truth."

—John 1:14

NOTES AND GUIDES

The lessons were designed to guide the reader without additional resources. However, leaders might find the aids below helpful in guiding discussions and provoking deeper contemplation.

LESSON ONE: WHEN GOD SPEAKS, WE SHOULD BELIEVE

Zechariah, an ordinary priest, was groomed in the teaching and ways of the Old Testament. The announcement of God's miraculous gift of a child should not have been met with doubt. Because he had been praying for a son so many years and had no answer from God, hesitations grew toward God's Word. For this reason, he was suspicious and disbelieving.

- **GENESIS 17:17** — Then Abraham fell on his face and laughed and said to himself, "Shall a child be born to a man who is a hundred years old? Shall Sarah, who is ninety years old, bear a child?"

- **GENESIS 18:11** — Now Abraham and Sarah were old, advanced in years. The way of women had ceased to be with Sarah.

- **GENESIS 30:23** — She [Rachel] conceived and bore a son and said, "God has taken away my reproach."

- **RICHARD SIBBES** — There are no men more careful of the use of means than those that are assured of a good issue and conclusion, for the one stirs up diligence in the other. Assurance of the end stirs up diligence in the means. For the soul of a believing Christian knows that God has decreed both.

LESSON TWO: WHEN GOD SPEAKS, WE SHOULD TRUST

While God's Word came to Zechariah as a favorable solution to his public shame of barrenness, it did not come so favorably to Mary. For her, the shame was about to begin. And, once the shame was gone and the child was born, further hurt would come as her son would soon be the most hated man in the region. Even still, she trusted God's Word.

- **GENESIS 3:15** — I will put enmity between you and the woman, and between your offspring and her offspring; he shall bruise your head, and you shall bruise his heel.

- **ISAIAH 14:27** — For the Lord of hosts has purposed, and who will annul it? His hand is stretched out, and who will turn it back?

- **RICHARD SIBBES** — We should answer God's dealing by our dealing. He works by contraries; we should judge by contraries. Therefore, if we be in misery, hope and wait for glory, in death look for life, in sense of sin assure thyself of pardon, for God's nature and promises are unchangeable; and when God will forgive, he lets us see our troubles. Therefore with resolute Job say, 'Though he kills me, I will yet trust in him.'

LESSON THREE: WHEN GOD SPEAKS, WE SHOULD WORSHIP

The parallels between the stories of Zechariah and Mary are unmistakable. Yet, they indicate how differently ordinary people like ourselves respond to extraordinary truth from God. If we are not careful, our situations will influence our thinking and weaken our faith in God's Word. A proper and faithful response to God's truth should be overwhelming excitement that moves us to worship with others in like mind. When we worship with others, our hearts are unified in Christ and our souls are encouraged.

- **JOB 5:8-11** — As for me, I would seek God, and to God would I commit my cause, who does great things and unsearchable, marvelous things without number: he gives rain on the earth and sends waters on the fields; he sets on high those who are lowly, and those who mourn are lifted to safety.

- **PSALM 98:3** — He has remembered his steadfast love and faithfulness to the house of Israel. All the ends of the earth have seen the salvation of our God.

- **PSALM 103:13** — As a father shows compassion to his children, so the Lord shows compassion to those who fear him.

- **PSALM 111:9** — He sent redemption to his people; he has commanded his covenant forever. Holy and awesome is his name!

- **RICHARD BAXTER** — Remember the perfections of that God whom you worship, that he is a Spirit, and therefore to be worshipped in spirit and truth; and that he is most great and terrible, and therefore to be worshipped with seriousness and reverence, and not to be dallied with, or served with toys or lifeless lip-service; and that he is most holy, pure, and jealous, and therefore to be purely worshipped; and that he is still present with you, and all things are naked and open to him with whom we have to do. The knowledge of God, and the remembrance of his all-seeing presence, are the most powerful means against hypocrisy.

GOD BREAKS HIS SILENCE

FOR DEVOTIONAL READING

BEFORE THE FIRST CHRISTMAS

The "silent treatment" can be brutal. We've all experienced it before. Some of us have dished it out. It's what happens when you upset someone so much that to speak would be the end of you.

The Israelites experienced it as a nation. God was silent for several generations, not because He was angry, but because He was rolling up His sleeves preparing the greatest speech in human history —the incarnation of the living Word.

The Israelites had a long past with God's word. He spoke to them through clouds, bushes, fire, prophets, patriarchs, kings, and more. The writer of Hebrews said, "Long ago, at many times and in many ways, God spoke to our fathers by the prophets, but in these last days he has spoken to us by his Son" (Heb. 1:1-2). With the appearing of Jesus, we have God's ultimate self-expression. "He is the radiance of the glory of God and the exact imprint of his nature," Hebrews continues (Heb. 1:3). When Jesus was born, God spoke most powerfully.

But our story begins several hundred years before Christ. The gospel had been unfolding since God's promise concerning Eve and the serpent in the garden some 4,000 years prior (Gen. 3:15). But rather than eagerly anticipating the promise fulfillment, the nation of Israel had grown spiritually cold. Their obedience had evolved to ritualistic chores and their affections had turned toward the world. "Why are we wasting our time serving God?" (*paraphrased*, Mal. 3:14). They had failed to give God their heart.

The story of God's redemption was grinding to a climactic halt. Malachi captured the Lord's shocking words:

"Behold, I will send you Elijah the prophet before the great and awesome day of the LORD comes. And he will turn the hearts of fathers to their children and the hearts of children to their fathers, lest I come and strike the land with a decree of utter destruction." (Mal. 4:5-6)

Then, God went silent.

Those were the final words of the final book of Scripture. It was a frightening cliffhanger. God was sending a herald to prepare the hearts of the people so that when the Lord came, He would not wipe them all out for their hard hearts. And swiftly, God hushed ... for 400 years.

Despite the warning, things continued spiraling downward as you would expect. Typically when the teacher is gone, the students act badly. The Israelites were no exception. It's no wonder God sent someone to prepare the way for His holy Son.

The wait was tough. Israel had grown accustomed to God's interaction. But He had not miraculously intervened in 800 years. No angels had appeared in 500 years. And now, no prophet had spoken for 400 years. It was all crickets for the Jews.

God was not stubbornly quiet to spite His people. He hadn't run out of things to reveal. He didn't get distracted or lose His tongue. He purposely withdrew Himself for His own purposes.

But now, He was about to break His silence.

PART 1

GOD HAS SPOKEN & WE SHOULD BELIEVE

It was a bloody mess. Blood on the floor. Blood on the walls. Blood on the garments. Jews from all over the known world were coming to the temple, as was their custom, to offer animal sacrifices to God—a picture to prepare them for the Messiah's work on the cross.

The priests would receive the animal and butcher it, separating specific parts of its body for specific purposes of worship in the temple. It would be burned, poured over coals, and surrendered to God in prayer. It was a scene of death.

There were about 18,000 priests at that time, divided across 24 divisions. Twice a year, a division would serve seven days in the temple. Doing the math, 750 priests were performing their duties on any given day. Out of those, only one would be privileged to carry the bloody, burning coals into the Holy Place. They drew straws to choose that person. It was the opportunity of a lifetime, literally. A priest could enter the Holy Place only once.

Our story introduces Zechariah. He is that privileged priest, that randomly chosen, insignificant man who just happened to be doing his job the day God broke His silence. He was a common man. In fact, he was one of 18,000 priests who were just like him. On the surface, there was nothing extraordinary about him being chosen for the job. It was in the straws.

A COMMON PRIEST

Nothing about Zechariah was extraordinary. The Bible tells us he was an old priest with no children—which made him a sham of a man among the people (Ps. 127:3). He was one in a million, but in a bad way.

In God's opinion, however, Zechariah and his wife, Elizabeth, were "righteous before God" (Lk. 1:6). This meant they didn't simply go through the motions of worship. Their hearts were in it. They were "Old Testament Christians," you might say.

Priests who entered the Holy Place would dress in a robe with bells that would ring with each step he took. A rope was tied to his ankle. The idea was if the bells stopped ringing, the priest was assumed dead and could be dragged out by his foot. Those who offered the sacrifices would gather around outside to pray until the priest returned.

> In the days of Herod, king of Judea, there was a priest named Zechariah, of the division of Abijah. And he had a wife from the daughters of Aaron, and her name was Elizabeth. And they were both righteous before God, walking blamelessly in all the commandments and statutes of the Lord. But they had no child, because Elizabeth was barren, and both were advanced in years.
>
> Now while he was serving as priest before God when his division was on duty, according to the custom of the priesthood, he was chosen by lot to enter the temple of the Lord and burn incense. And the whole multitude of the people were praying outside at the hour of incense. And there appeared to him an angel of the Lord standing on the right side of the altar of incense. And Zechariah was troubled when he saw him, and fear fell upon him. (Lk. 1:5-12)

AN UNCOMMON WORD

Zechariah was a common man, just like you and me. Being a priest was nothing extraordinary. He didn't work his way into the priesthood. He was born into it. He had no choice, neither was he awarded the duty of offering in the Holy Place. God picked a common man for an uncommon purpose—to receive an uncommon word—and broke His silence.

Typically, people did one of three things when they encountered an angel: they died, they ran, or they feared deeply. The Holy Place had only one entrance. Gabriel could not have been a man who just "appeared" inside. So upon seeing him, Zechariah was troubled. He wondered if the bells on his robe were about stop ringing.

> But the angel said to him, "Do not be afraid, Zechariah, for your prayer has been heard, and your wife Elizabeth will bear you a son, and you shall call his name John. And you will have joy and gladness, and many will rejoice at his birth, for he will be great before the Lord. And he must not drink wine or strong drink, and he will be filled with the Holy Spirit, even from his mother's womb. And he will turn many of the children of Israel to the Lord their God, and he will go before him in the spirit and power of Elijah, to turn the hearts of the fathers to the children, and the disobedient to the wisdom of the just, to make ready for the Lord a people prepared."
>
> And Zechariah said to the angel, "How shall I know this? For I am an old man, and my wife is advanced in years." And the angel answered him, "I am Gabriel. I stand in the presence of God, and I was sent to speak to you and to bring you this good news. And behold, you will be silent and unable to speak until the day that these things take place, because you did not believe my words, which will be fulfilled in their time." And the people were waiting for Zechariah, and they were wondering at his delay in the temple. And when he came out, he was unable to speak to them, and they realized that he had seen a vision in the temple. And he kept making signs to them and remained mute. And when his time of service was ended, he went to his home. (Lk. 1:13-23)

When God Speaks, We Should Believe

Zechariah, physically and emotionally drained, from years of priestly duties and unanswered prayers for a son, disbelieved God's Word. As a result, the angel struck him mute and deaf (Lk. 1:62-63), a serious punishment for a man who wanted to tell all about his wife's pregnancy.

Hebrews 1:2 tells us God speaks to us today through His living Word, and it is no less significant than if it came from an angel directly to you. Whenever and however God speaks, it is always Scripture. How do you typically respond to God's Word?

With the coming of Christmas, consider your response when God speaks—is it belief or disbelief?

PART 2

GOD HAS SPOKEN & WE SHOULD TRUST

The wind blew gently that afternoon as it did so many others. Nothing about it was extraordinary. It was just a usual day full of usual happenings. A young Jewish girl named Mary was grinding wheat and barley into flour, preparing food for the evening. Her father was off to work, her siblings tending to chores, and her mother away at the market.

Although alone at the house, no one was concerned about her safety. It was a small town with little noise, only the sound of young children playing and running about. There were only 2,000 souls in the whole city. You could easily miss it passing by in a caravan. Luke referred to it as Galilee. People knew Galilee. But this place, Nazareth, where was that?

Israel had not heard from God in 400 years. There had been no angelic appearances in 500 years, and no miracles in 800 years. Not until sixth months ago when Gabriel appeared to Zechariah, gave him God's Word and a miraculous conception. Now, on this usual day in this usual city as this usual girl was tending to her usual chores, God would do it again. This time, an even more miraculous conception would occur.

A COMMON GIRL

"Can anything good come out of Nazareth?" Nathanael asked, when Philip told him about Christ (Jn. 1:46). Nazareth was such an agricultural place and not particularly known for anything good. It was plain. So plain that not even a fisherman thought anything worth while would come out of it.

Mary, a teenage girl, was the only thing competing with Nazareth for insignificance. She lived in it. Her four letter name was so common in her day that we have more than seven in the New Testament alone. Luke tells us Zechariah was "righteous before God" (Lk. 1:6). But of Mary, he only says she was a virgin (Lk. 1:27). In the same verse, Luke says more about Mary's husband-to-be than her.

When the angel appeared to this common girl, she was not in the temple performing dignified priestly duties. Rather, she was at home making dinner. No one was relying on her for any spiritual purposes, only the work of her hands. And there were only a few who needed that.

> In the sixth month the angel Gabriel was sent from God to a city of Galilee named Nazareth, to a virgin betrothed to a man whose name was Joseph, of the house of David. And the virgin's name was Mary. And he came to her and said, "Greetings, O favored one, the Lord is with you!" (Lk. 1:26-28)

AN UNCOMMON WORD

Mary must have had her back to the angel when he spoke because it was his greeting that troubled her, not his appearance. "Greetings, O favored one, the Lord is with you!" This was not your typical "hello"!

Describing her as "favored one" was pretty significant. It didn't imply that she had or did anything in particular to warrant God's goodness. Rather, it implied that God, out of His goodness, wanted her to be favored. He intended to make her the mother of our Lord. Now that is significant!

God broke His silence yet again. This time, the word was that she would have a son and name Him Jesus. He would not be a common boy. He would be the "Son of the Most High" and "of his kingdom there will be no end" (Lk. 1:31-33). Gabriel explained how it would happen (Lk. 1:35) because nothing is impossible with God (Lk. 1:37). In this promise, Mary simply trusted. "Let it be to me according to your word," she said. No objections. No complaints. Mary trusted God's Word.

> But she was greatly troubled at the saying, and tried to discern what sort of greeting this might be. And the angel said to her, "Do not be afraid, Mary, for you have found favor with God. And behold, you will conceive in your womb and bear a son, and you shall call his name Jesus. He will be great and will be called the Son of the Most High. And the Lord God will give to him the throne of his father David, and he will reign over the house of Jacob forever, and of his kingdom there will be no end."
>
> And Mary said to the angel, "How will this be, since I am a virgin?"
>
> And the angel answered her, "The Holy Spirit will come upon you, and the power of the Most High will overshadow you; therefore the child to be born will be called holy—the Son of God. And behold, your relative Elizabeth in her old age has also conceived a son, and this is the sixth month with her who was called barren. For nothing will be impossible with God." And Mary said, "Behold, I am the servant of the Lord; let it be to me according to your word." And the angel departed from her. (Lk. 1:29-38)

WHEN GOD SPEAKS, WE SHOULD TRUST

Mary, a lowly Jewish girl from an undistinguished town, modeled the proper way to respond to God's Word—with faith. Although she knew it was extraordinary, she trusted God to make possible the impossible conception of a child in her womb. She was graced by God to be favored for all time.

How do you respond to God's Word when you hear or read it? Do you trust in His promises when reality says otherwise? Do you stand confidently and lean into the unknown? God can do the impossible. When He says He will do something, He will do it because nothing thwarts His plan (Is. 14:27).

With Christmas coming, consider how you will respond when God speaks—is it with doubt or faith?

PART 3

GOD HAS SPOKEN & WE SHOULD WORSHIP

The excitement was too much. Mary left home as soon as she was able. Elizabeth was sixth months pregnant, and seeing Elizabeth would increase her faith and allow her to celebrate God's grace. Mary believed His word and trusted. She didn't need confirmation. She needed spiritual strength.

Unlike Elizabeth, whose reproach among people would be lifted by God's word, Mary knew that reproach was coming because she was unmarried and expecting a baby. Nevertheless, this was thrilling news. She needed to see her pregnant cousin.

This was an extraordinary time. Not only was the long anticipated Christ coming, He was making His way through these rather common people. The red carpet was being rolled out. But there were no cameras, no lights, no press conferences. There was only a mention in the ears of a virgin girl, an old man, and his barren wife.

Even in these trifling events, God broke His silence in a spectacular way. It was the first miracle in nearly a millennium, the first angelic appearance in half a millennium, and the first time God had spoken in several generations. It was all happening at once. And yet, it was nothing compared to the thunderous Word that would be born into this world.

A COMMON NEED

The stories of Zechariah and Mary are strikingly parallel. Both involved common people being interrupted by an angelic visitation while doing their common duties. Both are greeted by Gabriel and deeply troubled. They were both told, "Do not be afraid," and both promised a son. The promised sons were both considered unusually great. Zechariah and Mary responded to the angel with questions. The angel gave them both signs, and both were extraordinarily blessed for the sake of blessing the world.

Mary, desiring to affirm and strengthen her trust, rushed to Elizabeth's house. And, while greeting her, baby John leaped in the womb—no doubt meeting his destiny as the herald of the Messiah. It was as if he was pointing and telling, "The Savior is here!" How could he do that? Because God said, "he will be filled with the Holy Spirit, even from his mother's womb" (Lk. 1:16).

His mother, exuding with joy and also filled with the Holy Spirit, realized what had happened and burst out a prophetic word of blessing. She blessed Mary, blessed Jesus, blessed herself, and blessed all who believe the Word of God (Lk. 1:42-45). Mary, also overwhelmed by it all, cried out in a song of worship, magnifying the Lord for His mercy and grace on the humble, His strength and might above all people, and for keeping His promise made 4,000 years prior.

> In those days Mary arose and went with haste into the hill country, to a town in Judah, and she entered the house of Zechariah and greeted Elizabeth. And when Elizabeth heard the greeting of Mary, the baby leaped in her womb. And Elizabeth was filled with the Holy Spirit, and she exclaimed with a loud cry, "Blessed are you among women, and blessed is the fruit of your womb! And why is this granted to me that the mother of my Lord should come to me? For behold, when the sound of your greeting came to my ears, the baby in my womb leaped for joy. And blessed is she who believed that there would be a fulfillment of what was spoken to her from the Lord." (Lk. 1:39-45)

AN UNCOMMON WORD

The stories of Zechariah and Mary also had some differences. Some were more obvious than others. For instance, Zechariah was an old man. Mary was a young girl. Zechariah was married in need of a child. Mary was single and not seeking a child. Zechariah had a lifetime to cultivate his faith. Mary only had several years. Zechariah's promise would lift his reproach among people. Mary's would bring her reproach among people. Zechariah didn't believe. Mary did.

More subtle differences are found when you look more closely. Zechariah's son would be great among people. Mary's son would be the epitome of great. Zechariah's son would point to the Christ. Mary's son would be the Christ.

Mary and Elizabeth's shared joy was overwhelming. They were both caught up in adoration of the Lord. It was a spiritually rich time. Zechariah, made deaf and mute, would not have heard the loud bursts of his wife and cousin. So Mary followed Elizabeth's prophetic blessing with "The Magnificat," as it is commonly called today. It is the summary of the spirit of Christmas—the Lord's promised gift now given to the world.

> And Mary said, "My soul magnifies the Lord, and my spirit rejoices in God my Savior, for he has looked on the humble estate of his servant. For behold, from now on all generations will call me blessed; for he who is mighty has done great things for me, and holy is his name. And his mercy is for those who fear him from generation to generation. He has shown strength with his arm; he has scattered the proud in the thoughts of their hearts; he has brought down the mighty from their thrones and exalted those of humble estate; he has filled the hungry with good things, and the rich he has sent away empty. He has helped his servant Israel, in remembrance of his mercy, as he spoke to our fathers, to Abraham and to his offspring forever." (Lk. 1:46-55)

When God Speaks, We Should Worship

These are stories of common folk just like you and me. Some of us are old and bruised by life. We've prayed for decades and seen no end. We've concluded that God is still silent. We've wondered if God is able. We've lost the connection with God's Word. We see it as mere paper—not the culminating picture of Jesus. So we don't read it.

The Scripture is God's Word. The Scripture is where God speaks (Heb. 1:1-2). When our hearts grow cold and our lives become dull, we question His truths, dispute His gifts, and distrust His promises. The gospel of John describes Jesus as the incarnate Word of God, the Word made flesh, the climactic message of God, the divine self-expression. He existed before creation and was introduced into creation (Jn. 1:1-18). This is the birth of Christ.

When the written Word is read, the living Word is seen. This Christmas, how will you read God's Word? Are you anticipating a profound break of silence as you reflect on the birth of the incarnate Word?

GOD BREAKS HIS SILENCE

ADDITIONAL RESOURCES

SMALL GROUP TOOL KIT

Hey, I know how important it is to use the visual arts to help spread the word for a new class or small group. So, I created a tool kit just for that. It is the *God Breaks His Silence: Small Group Tool Kit* and it is chalk full of resources to help you spread the word, enhance presentations, and even white label the lessons.

The kit comes with a number of graphic designs. There are several posters ready to print. You can white label them or leave as-is. Be sure to drop your date, time, and location, if you are using them to point people to your gathering. Do what you want with them. They come in common sizes, including 12 x 18 inches, 16 x 20 inches, 18 x 24 inches, and 24 x 36 inches. Mount or hang them on walls, slide them into frames, post them to bulletin boards, or drop them on desktops and counters. You decide.

Additionally, the kit contains the actual study guid material in a variety of formats. It is in a beautifully composed PDF in two sizes: one for print and one for emailing. It is also in a plain Microsoft Word document for you to change and format however you need to. (I only ask that you do not change the content.)

If you are in an auditorium or large room and plan to use multimedia, there are many HD sized slides at your disposal. The kit includes titles, lesson headings, scriptures, and blank slides for you to overlay whatever you want. Again, they are all HD quality.

If this is something you need, go to my website and download the tool kit for yourself: http://www.jacobabshire.com

JACOB ABSHIRE

Hi. My name is Jacob Abshire and I am desperate for Jesus Christ. He is my way, truth, and life. My wife agrees—for herself, that is. She is equally desperate. Together, we love to call Him ours.

We also love to raise our four children to call on Jesus the same way. We live in Houston—the greatest "country" in the United States. We love to worship with our spiritual family at Northeast Houston Baptist Church.

My joy in life is to use creative means to bring others closer to God's word in order to find the riches of God's truth for the glory of God's son. In other words, I am "creatively making disciples." One of the ways I do this is by writing. First, I write at my personal blog (jacobabshire.com) where I turn up writings about church and family life, ministry, leadership, technology, scripture, and general musings. Second, I write books (because my friends pressure me to). In 2009, I published *Forgiveness: A Commentary on Philemon*. Three years later, I followed it up with *Faith: A Commentary on James*. Both are part of an ongoing series I call, "Reader's Commentaries," because they are comprehensive commentaries in a readable form. (One readers said that they are for people who hate to read but want to learn the Bible.) I also write small group discussion guides and design artwork consistent with my joy (all of which are available on my site).

For more information, visit my blog. If you have questions, shoot me a message on my contact page. I usually respond the same day. Grace and peace.

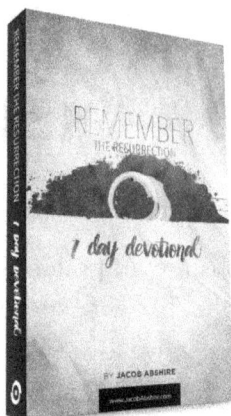

REMEMBER THE RESURRECTION

7 DAY DEVOTIONAL

How often do you remember the resurrection? After Jesus was crucified, His disciples were deeply troubled. They were saddened by His death. This is where we begin our devotional journey. We will ask ourselves as the angels asked Mary, "Why are you weeping?"

Then, we will follow along the story looking for more questions and inquiring them of ourselves, thinking more deeply about the resurrection and what it means for us today. We will join the disciples and seek in wonder, see in amazement, savor in understanding, satisfy in assurance, surrender in reverence, and finally, share in excitement.

Together, with the Holy Scriptures, we will go back in time, walk with the disciples, and personally reflect on the importance of the resurrection. My aim in this devotional series is to help you become more mindful of the resurrection through life lessons on faith.

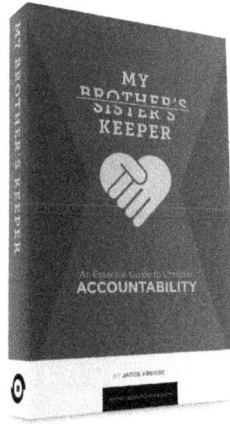

MY BROTHER'S KEEPER

AN ESSENTIAL GUIDE TO CHRISTIAN ACCOUNTABILITY

"Fortify your friends to mortify your sins." Stephen the Levite was right on target with those words. God tells us to "put to death what is earthly in you" (Col. 3:5). He says, "For if you live according to the flesh you will die, but if by the Spirit you put to death the deeds of the body, you will live" (Rom. 8:13).

Killing sin is not only a command, but a characteristic of the Christian. If we are "of Christ," we follow His Spirit, not the sinful world. Still, putting off the flesh and putting on Christ (Rom. 13:14) is not always easy alone. For this reason, God gave us each other. He gave us Christian accountability.

In *My Brother's Keeper: An Essential Guide to Christian Accountability*, I discuss the concept of teaming up to kill sin and practical ways to thrive in it. From meeting to mediating, this book provides the tools you need to fortify your friends and mortify your sins.

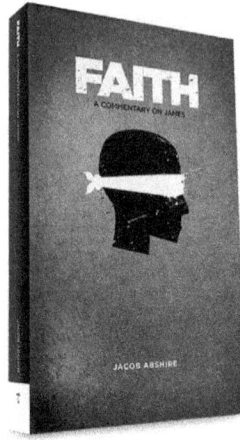

FAITH

A COMMENTARY ON JAMES

Do your troubles reveal faith that can save? In the Bible, James progresses through a series of troubles like the ones you face and ones you may not even know you face. He calls them trials. When our sinful lives collide against the holiness of God and our pride is smashed to pieces, we find the foremost gift of God as deposited in us by Christ. In our wreckage, we can learn to appreciate our troubles for what they are—divinely purposed trials that reveal and mature our belief in Christ. In this book, we will follow along with James and see what we can uncover about the foremost gift of God: Faith.

Find out why trials are our greatest gifts … This book explores 18 characteristics of faith in order to help you mature as a Christ follower. But before you can begin your journey, you must be ready and willing to let the waves wreck you again and again.

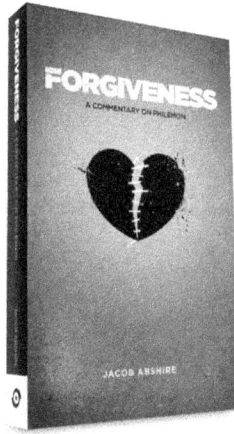

FORGIVENESS

A COMMENTARY ON PHILEMON

Despite its small size, the book of Philemon is quite colossal, theologically speaking. It instructs us on forgiveness and does so in a unique and practical way. And while it does this, it gently teaches on matters of equality, fellowship, edification and more. Only 25 verses long, it packs 25 chapters worth of divine guidance for us all.

In this book, we will unpack these divinities so that we can think and behave more like our Lord, who is a forgiving God (Ex. 34:6-7). Technically, this book is called a "commentary" on Philemon; however, it has been written in a way that is unlike typical commentaries, which often read like textbooks, focus on individual passages, and have a choppy flow. The flow of this book is fluid, transitioning from point to point, like topical books do. However, in this book all of the points are posited by scripture. This is a commentary for those who don't like commentaries.

www.ingramcontent.com/pod-product-compliance
Lightning Source LLC
Chambersburg PA
CBHW031629040426

42452CB00007B/744